ECASTER

14064

EnvyPak™

Fender Deluxe Reverb amp used in DVD courtesy of Rick Fuhry

ISBN 978-1-4803-5364-0

HAL•LEONARD®
CORPORATION
7777 W. BLUEMOUND RD. P.O. BOX 13819 MILWAUKEE, WI 53213

In Australia Contact:
Hal Leonard Australia Pty. Ltd.
4 Lentara Court
Cheltenham, Victoria, 3192 Australia
Email: ausadmin@halleonard.com.au

Visit Hal Leonard Online at
www.halleonard.com

Contents

Introduction

Thank you for taking the time to look into my point of view of the guitar! Every idea we have comes from someone or somewhere. Having said that, please do your best to keep in mind that these ideas are most definitely intended to be mended and sculpted into your own ideas on the fretboard. I've been fortunate enough to find endless amounts of joy from these concepts and I hope that you receive nothing short of the same! When any player of any genre finds a Telecaster in their hands, they are compelled to play guitar much differently than they usually would, regardless of the scenario. Some of the most inspiring ideas and sounds that musicians have ever heard have been created due to this unspoken relationship, and this should never die. I hope that anyone who aspires to find their own unique voice on the guitar will keep contributing to the massive collection of ideas we all pull from and share with each other each and every day. Never stop improving. Always be fearless. And always remember that it is all about the music! I am beyond honored that you have taken the time to let me show you some of my ideas and possibly help improve your musical knowledge. I hope that one day, I will learn ideas from you as well.

–Daniel Donato

How to Use This Book

The rhythm tab notation in this book matches the sequence of the performances and lessons on the accompanying DVD, so you can follow along and use for practice.

About the Author

Starting at just the age of 12, Daniel Donato has wasted no time in searching for his own unique voice on the guitar. Shortly after picking up the instrument, Daniel discovered his passion for older music—most of all, country and western. After doing so, he decided to dive into the live music scene in Nashville to assist in the development of his unique approach to the guitar. Through his studies of players from the past and present, along with hundreds of shows under his belt with the coveted Don Kelley Band, Daniel has become popular among musicians in the Nashville scene.

𝓣𝓻𝓪𝓲𝓷 𝓙𝓪𝓶

A

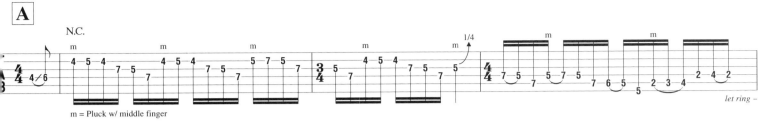

m = Pluck w/ middle finger

B

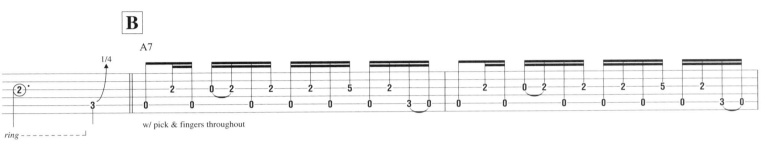

w/ pick & fingers throughout

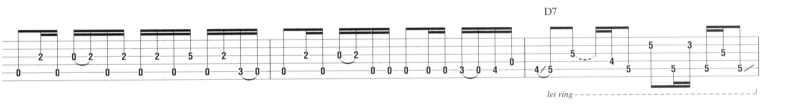

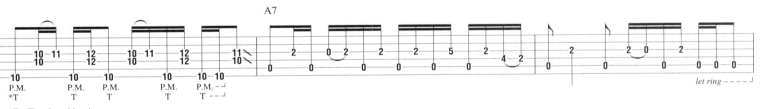

*T = Thumb on 6th string

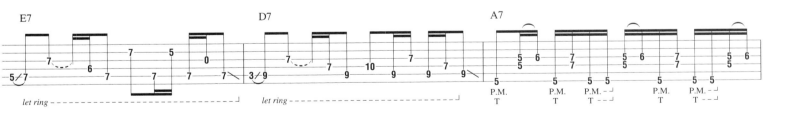

C

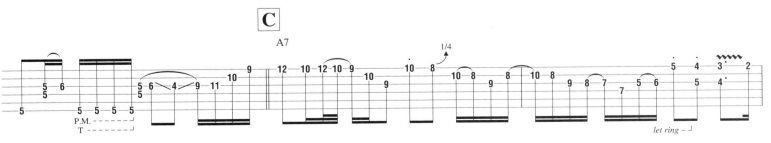

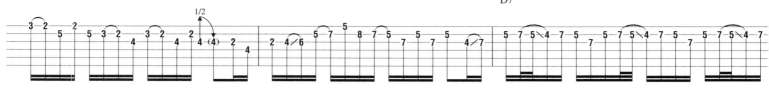

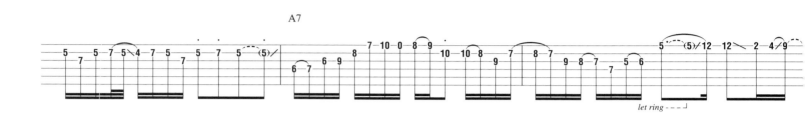

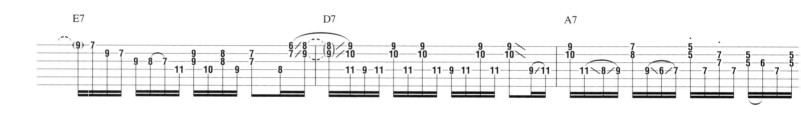

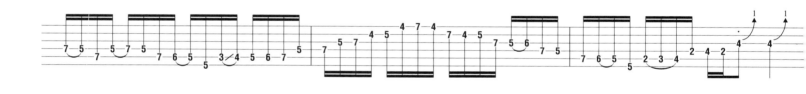

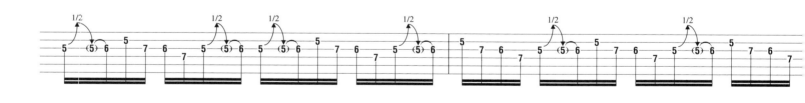

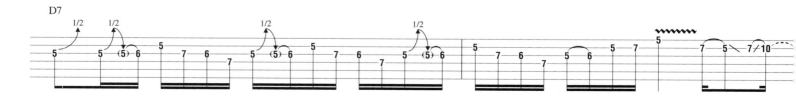

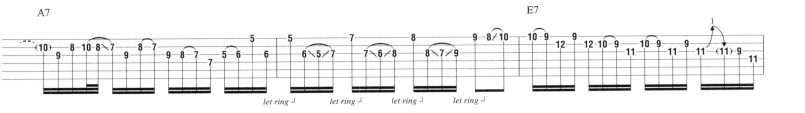

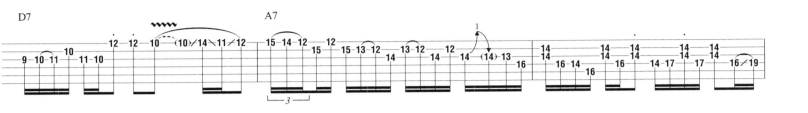

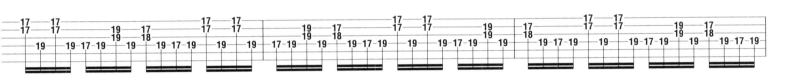

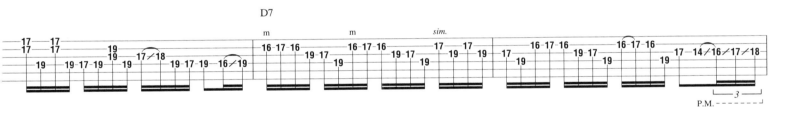

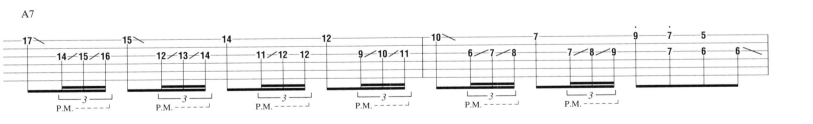

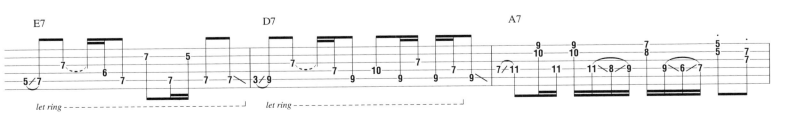

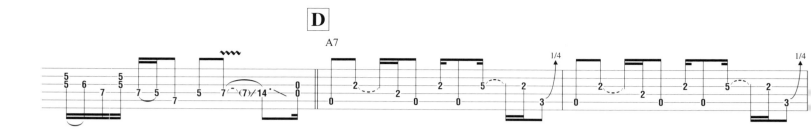

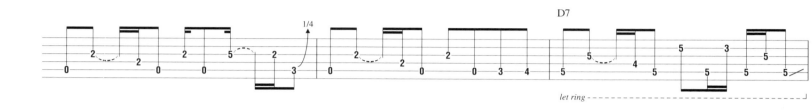

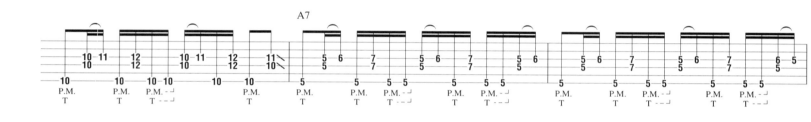

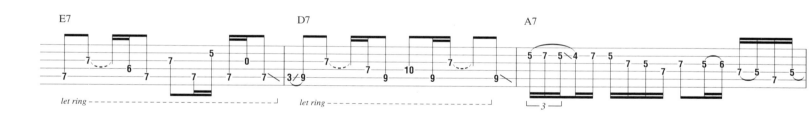

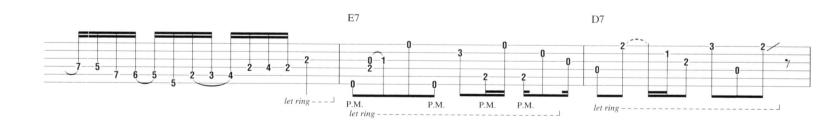

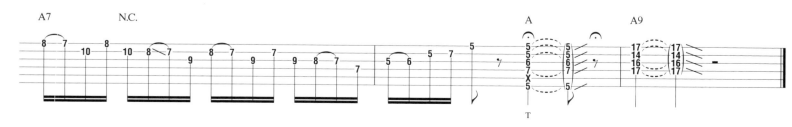

The Pathways

FIVE PATHWAYS IN A

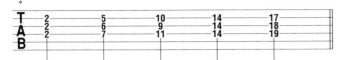

*All musical examples are played w/ pick & fingers unless indicated otherwise.

INVERSIONS

No Inversion   **2nd Inversion**   **1st Inversion**

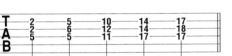

DOMINANT 7TH ADDED

Key of A   **Key of G**   **Key of C**

 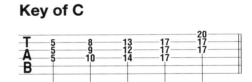

PRACTICE METHOD 1

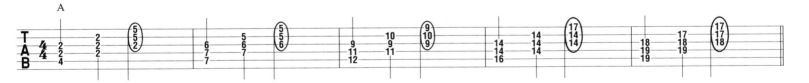

PRACTICE METHOD 2

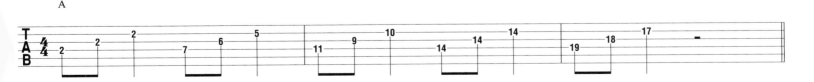

9

Chromatic Notes

CONNECTING PATHWAYS WITH CHROMATICS

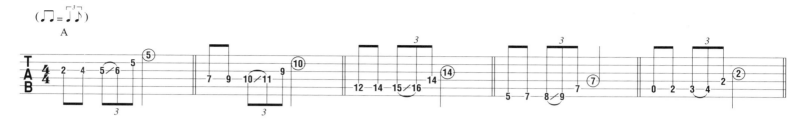

Adding ♭7

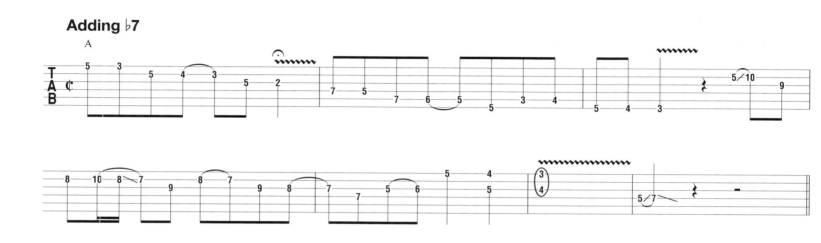

Adding ♭7 & ♭5

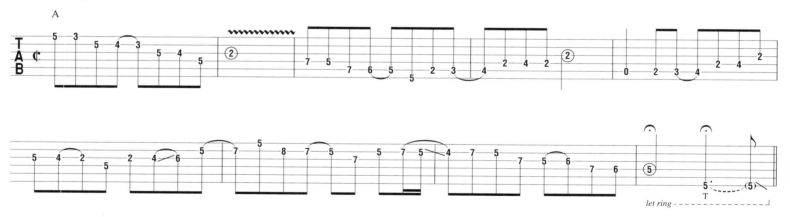

Ex. 1

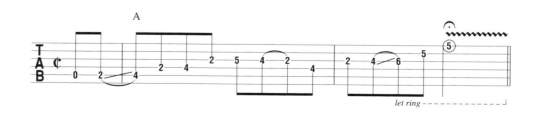

MORE CONNECTING PATHWAYS WITH CHROMATICS

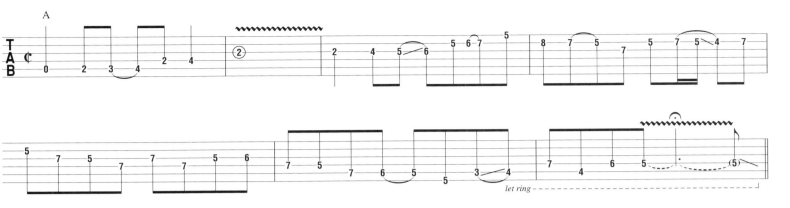

Ex. 2

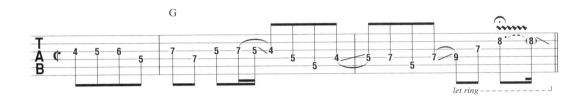

Ex. 2: Moving Down the Neck

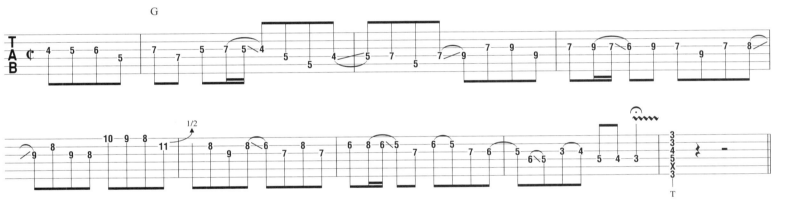

Ex. 2: Moving Up the Neck

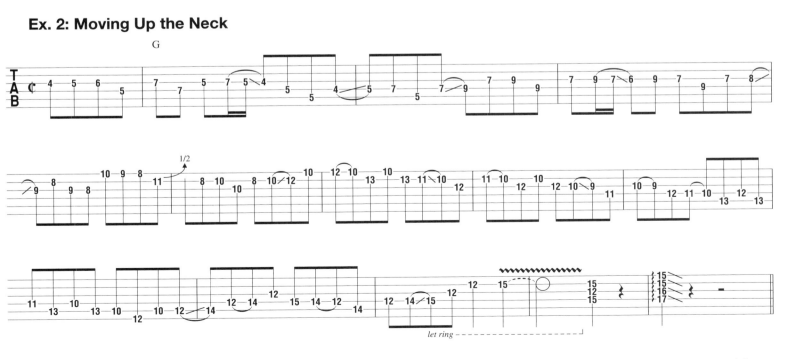

Ex. 3

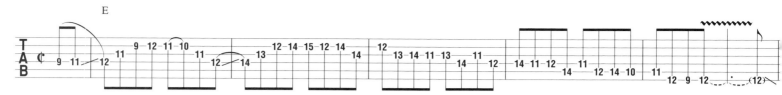

Ex. 3: Creating a New Lick

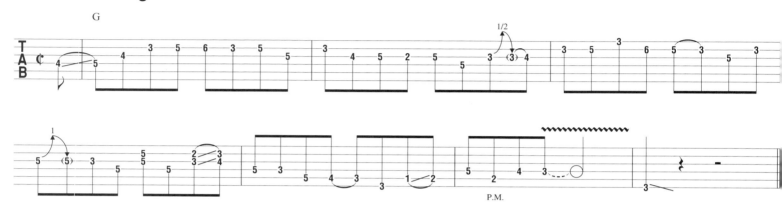

Ex. 3: Creating Another New Lick

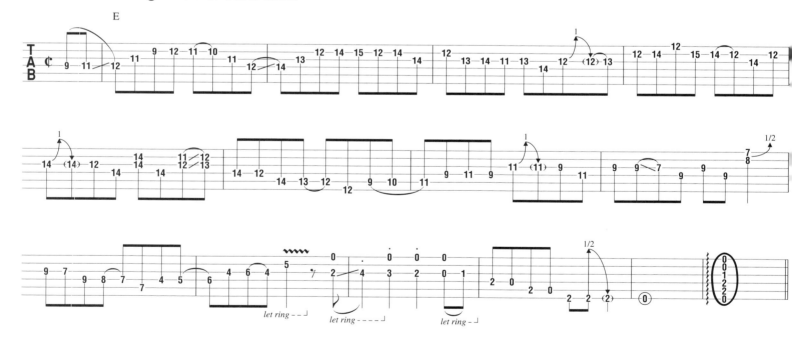

Application of Bends

Blues Style

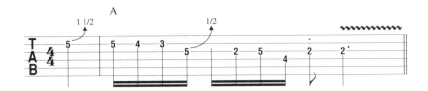

Clapton Style

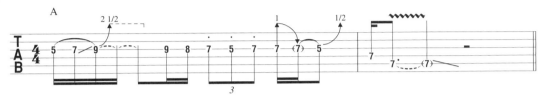

Bloomfield Style

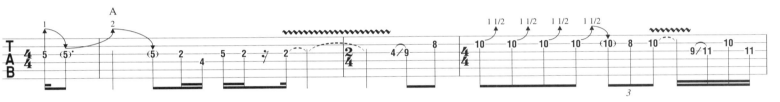

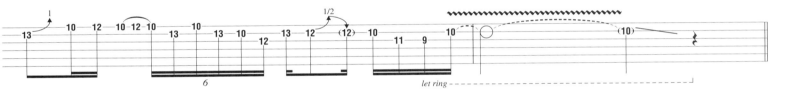

Country Style 1

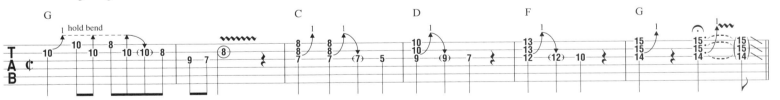

Country Style 2

Country Style 3

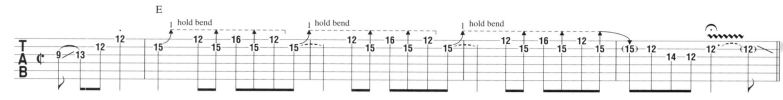

DANIEL'S BEND CONCEPTS

Ex. 1

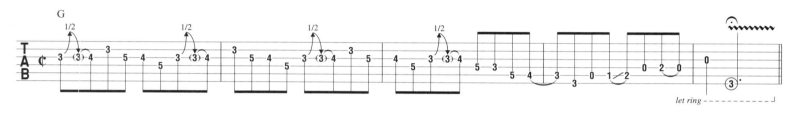

Ex. 1: Applied to a Blues Concept

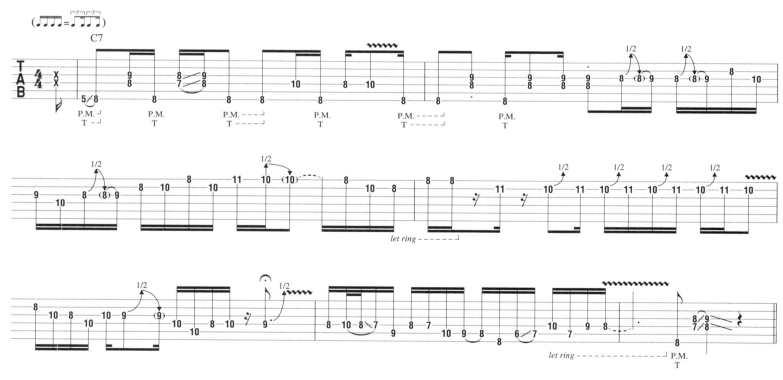

Ex. 1: Creating a New Idea

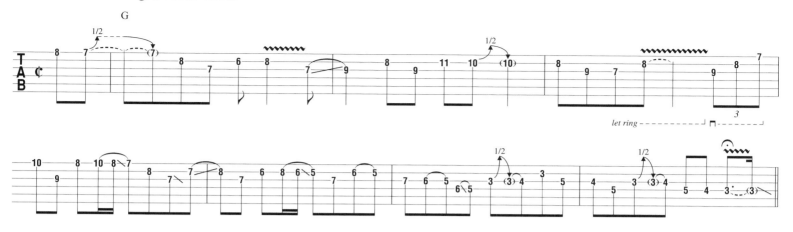

Ex. 2

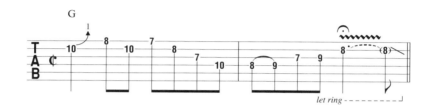

Ex. 2: In the Key of E

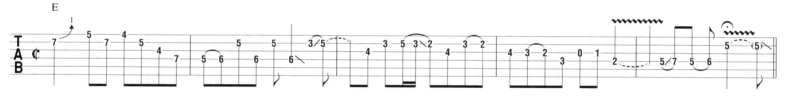

Ex. 3

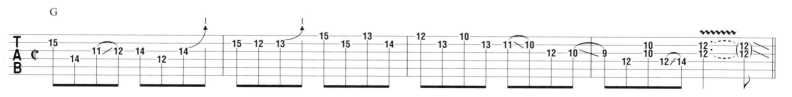

Double Stops

Ex. 1

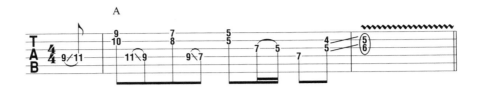

Ex. 1: Expanded Lick

Ex. 2

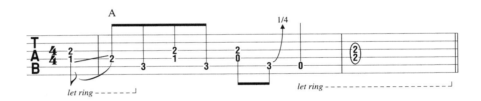

Ex. 1 & 2: Combined

JOHNNY HILAND'S COMPASS 1

COMPASS 2

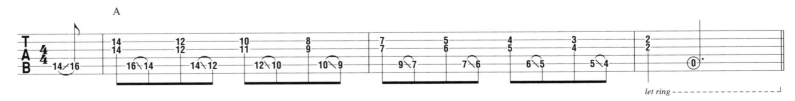

16

COMPASS 3

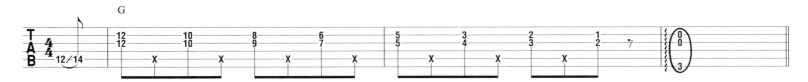

COMPASS 4

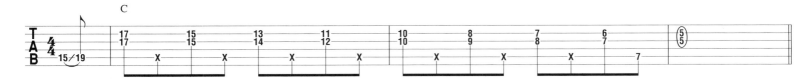

DANIEL'S COMPASS
Version 1

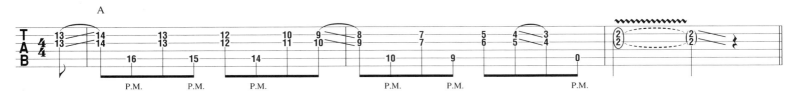

Version 2

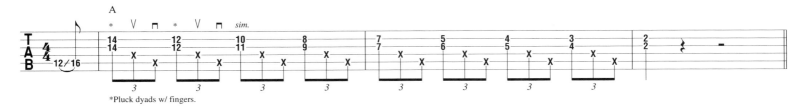

*Pluck dyads w/ fingers.

DANIEL'S DOUBLE-STOP CONCEPT

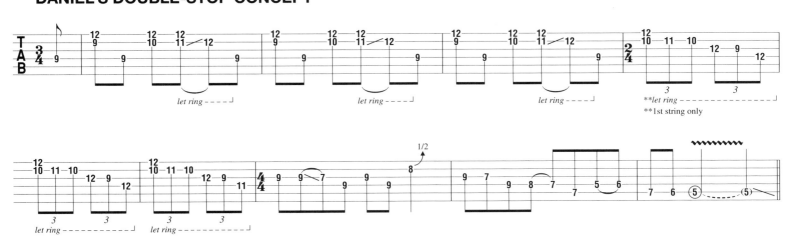

Smooth Pull-Off

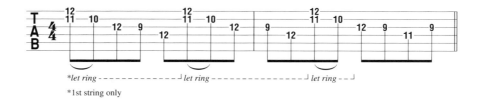

Smooth Pull-Off with Rhythm

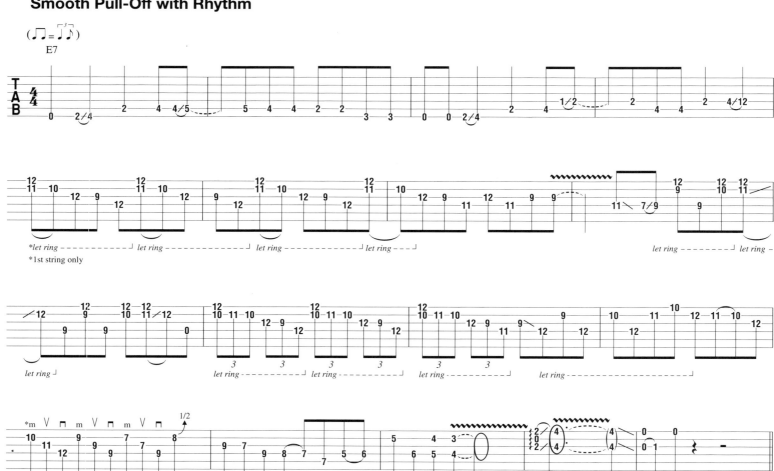

RHYTHMIC CONCEPT

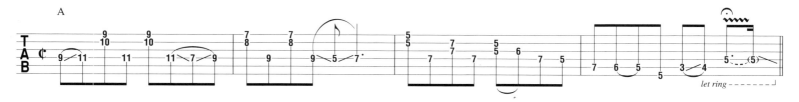

Note "Swinging"

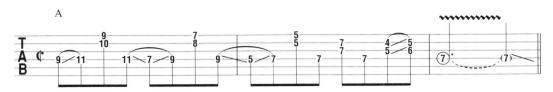

Fast Bluegrass Beat

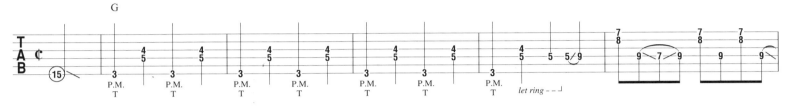

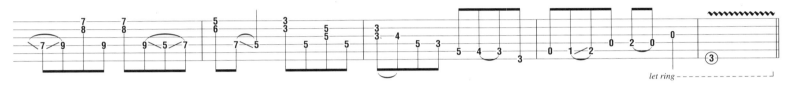

Funky Meters-Style Beat

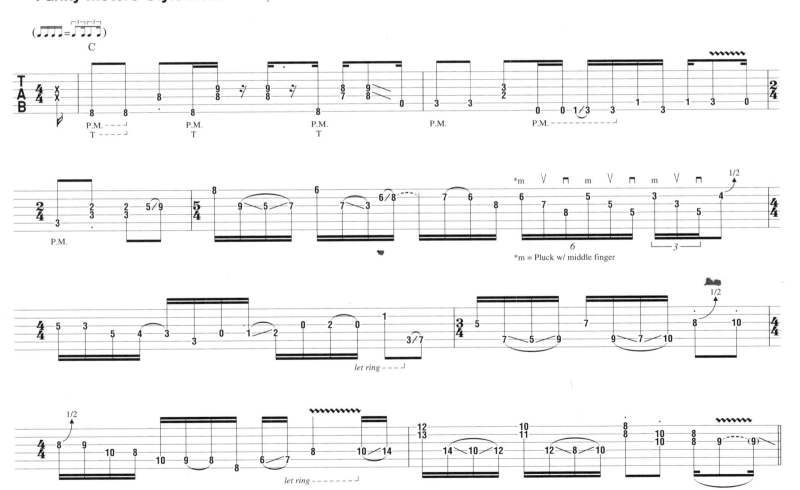

JAMES MITCHELL DOUBLE STOP

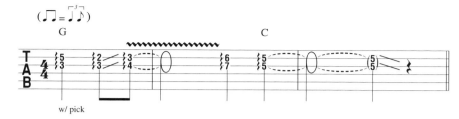

Shuffle

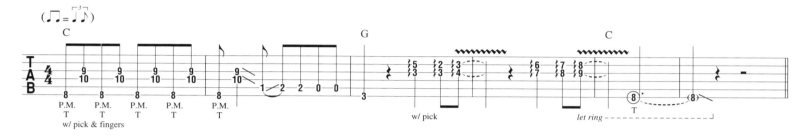

MOVING THROUGH A I–IV–V PROGRESSION

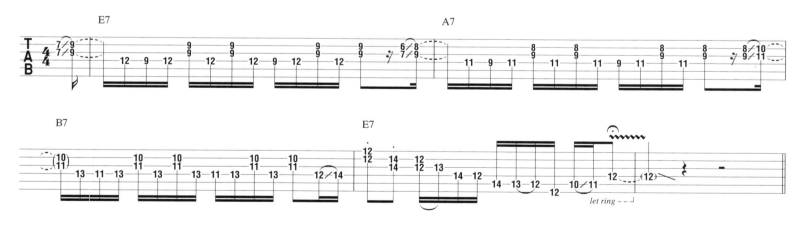

Incorporating Previous Techniques

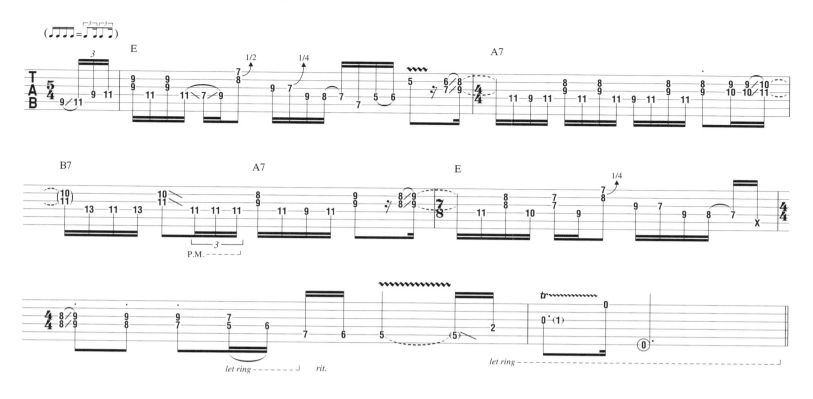

GHOST NOTE TECHNIQUE

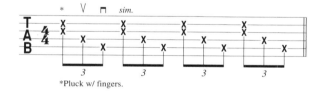

*Pluck w/ fingers.

Ghost Note Technique Application

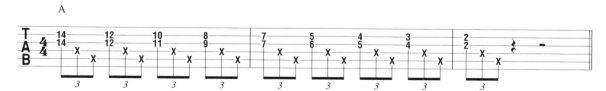

Analyzing Different Styles

J.D. SIMO

Bluesy & Chromatic 1

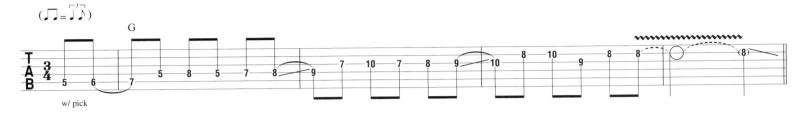

Bluesy & Chromatic 2

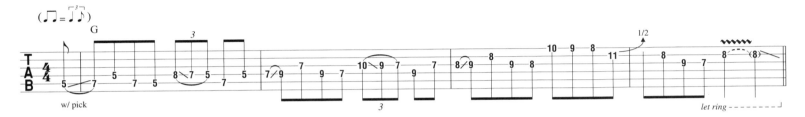

Moving Around the Neck

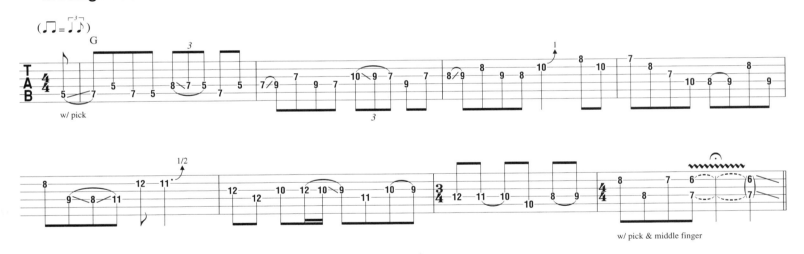

Bluesy Approach

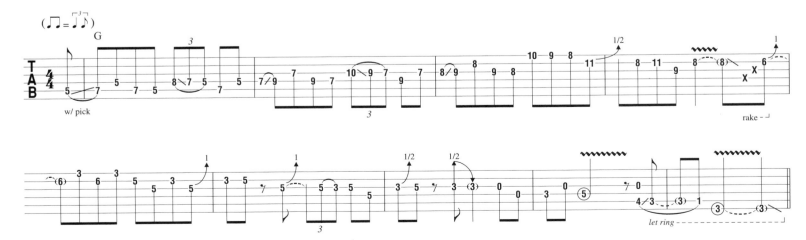

JAMES MITCHELL

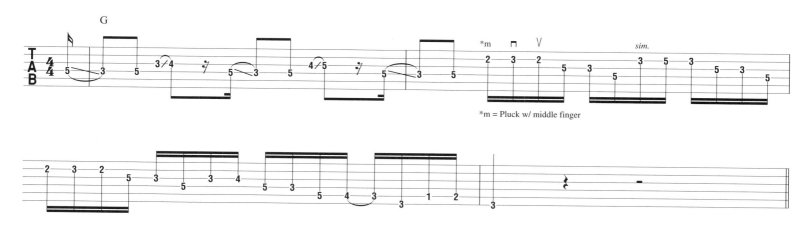

*m = Pluck w/ middle finger

Combining James and J.D.

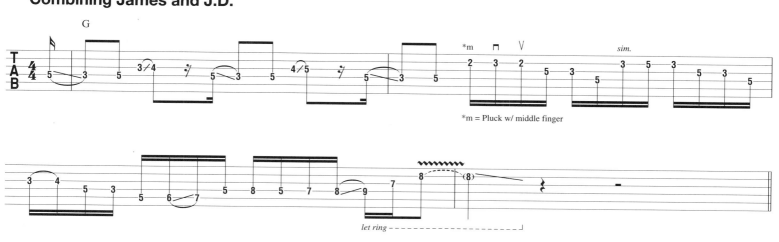

*m = Pluck w/ middle finger

let ring ─

RED VOLKAERT

Pedaling the 5th

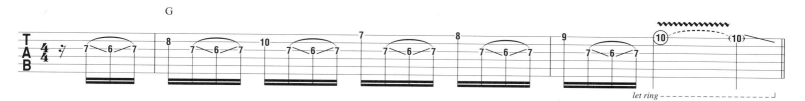

let ring ─ ─ ─ ─ ─ ─ ─ ─ ─ ─ ─ ─ ─ ─ ─ ─ ─

Moving Down the Neck

Moving Up the Neck

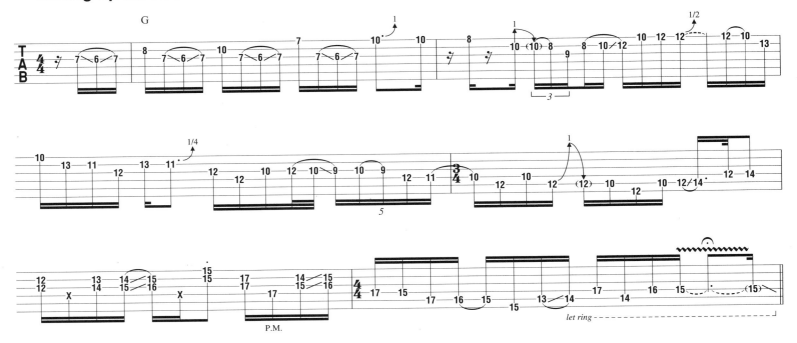

DANNY GATTON

Rapid-Fire

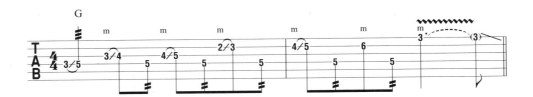

Higher Position

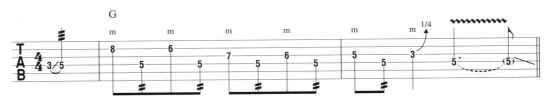

With Double Stops

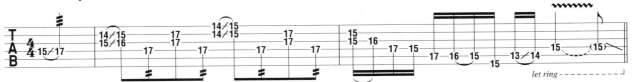

GRADY MARTIN

Jazzy Phrase

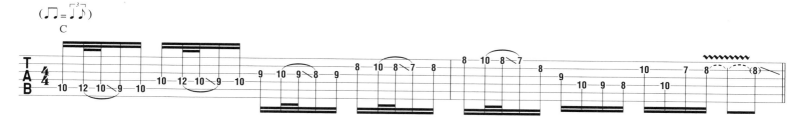

In a Slow Blues

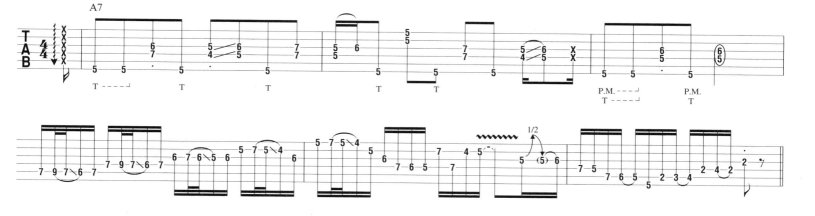

In a Fast Song

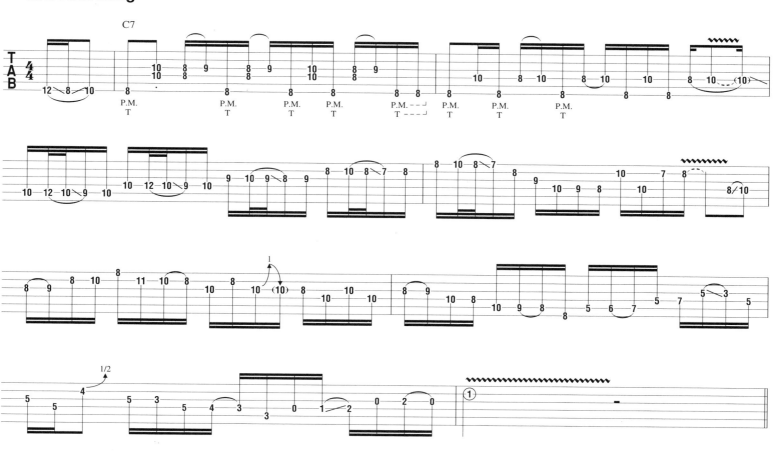

ROY NICHOLS

Interesting Note Choices

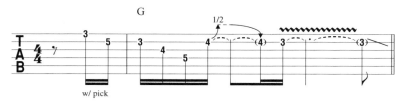

Chromatic Runs

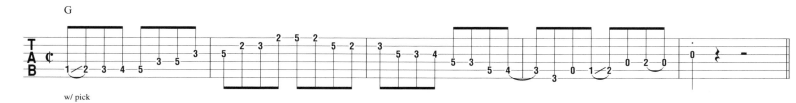

In a Fast Context

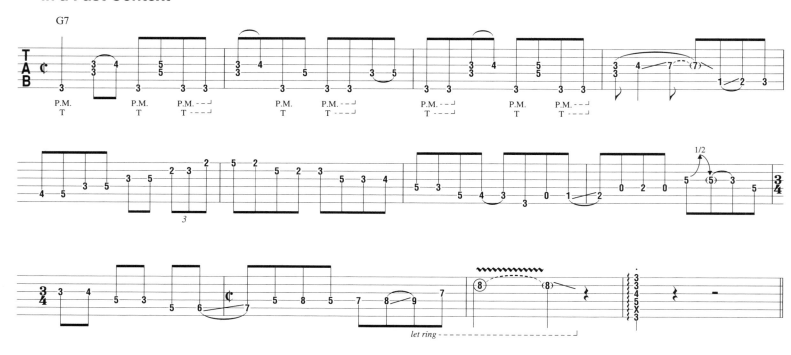

HANK GARLAND

Sweeping Phrase

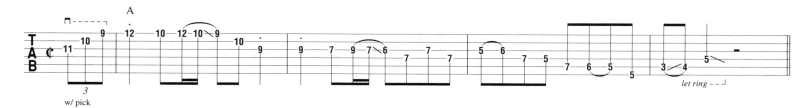

Repeated Figure

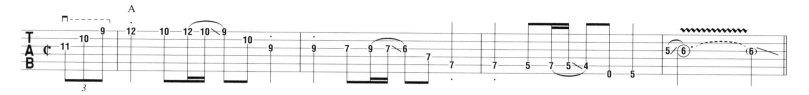

Moving Down the Neck in G

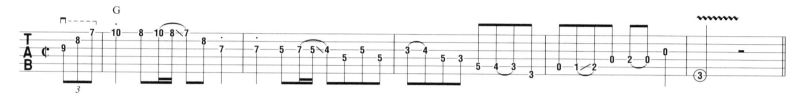

Moving Up the Neck

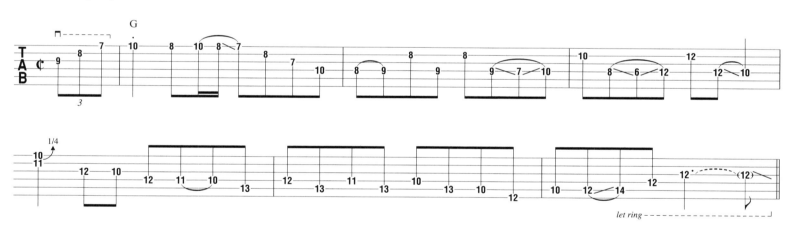

Blues Jam

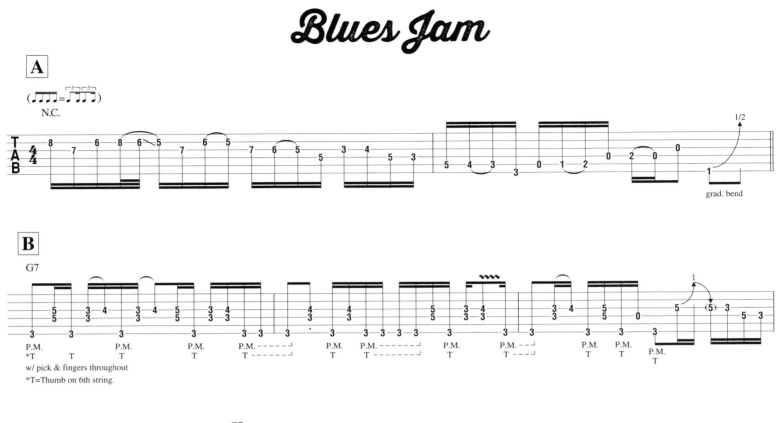

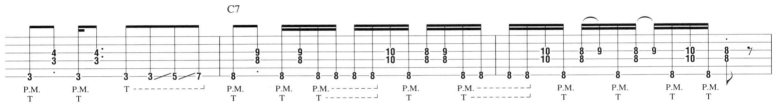

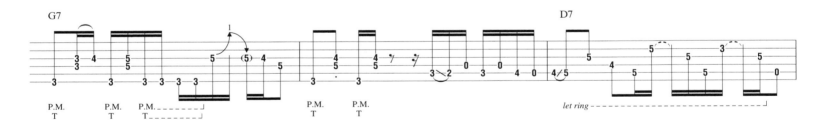

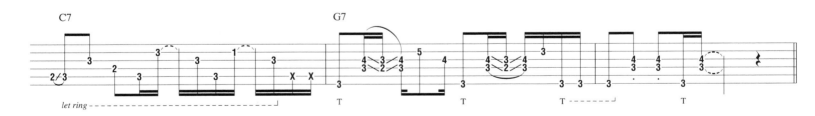

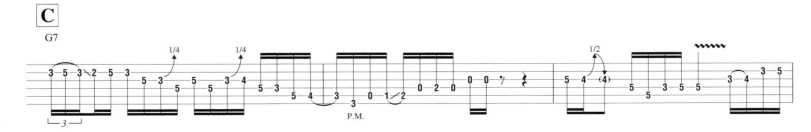

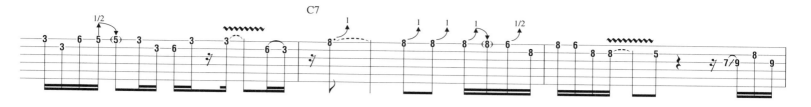

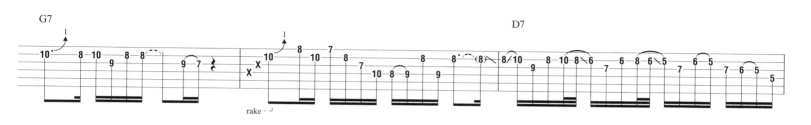

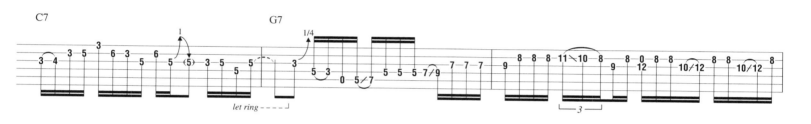

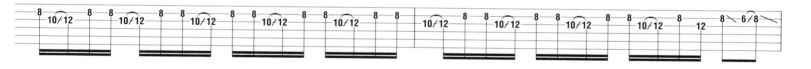

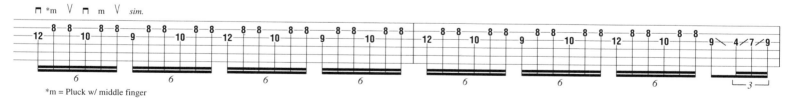

*m = Pluck w/ middle finger

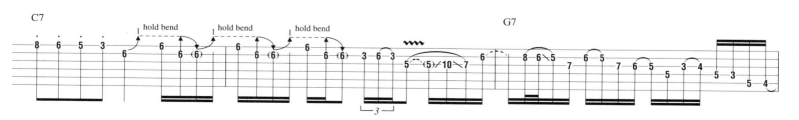

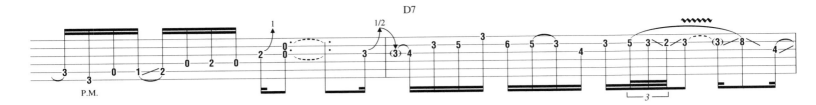

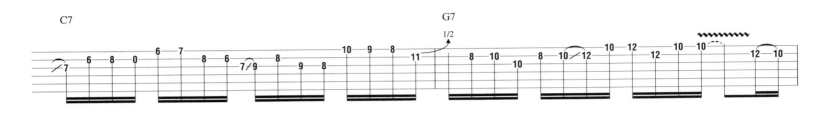

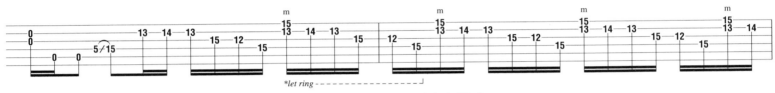

*let ring - - - - - - - - - - - - - - - -

*Refers to 1st string only, which is plucked w/ middle finger.

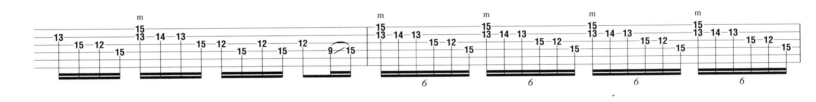

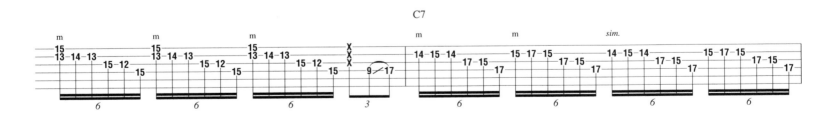

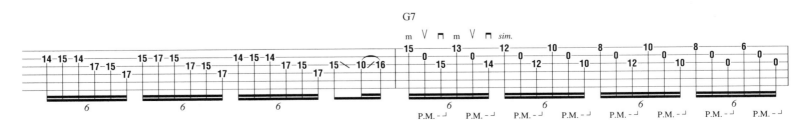

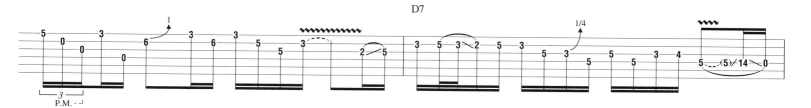

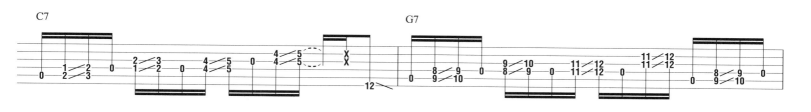

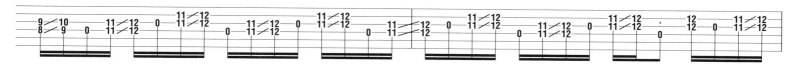

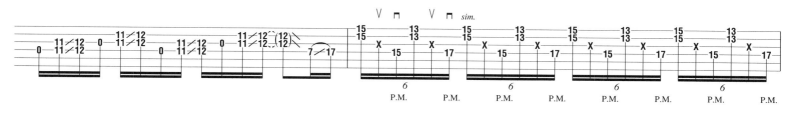

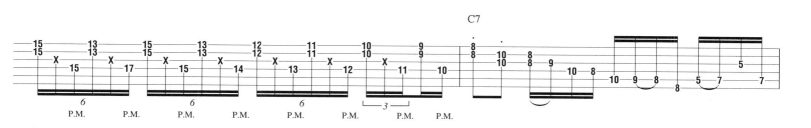

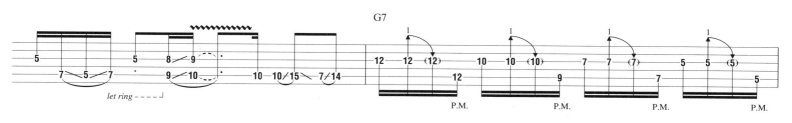

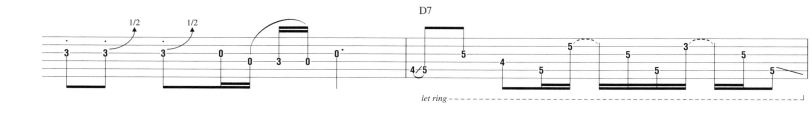

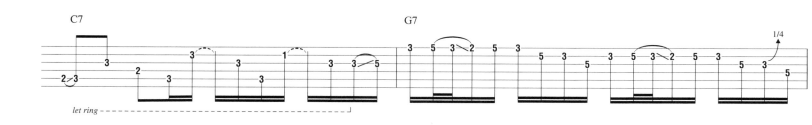

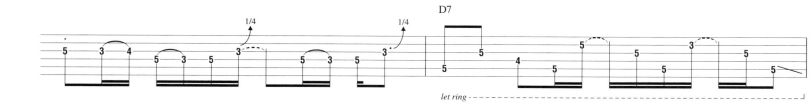

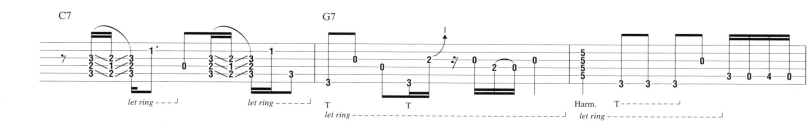

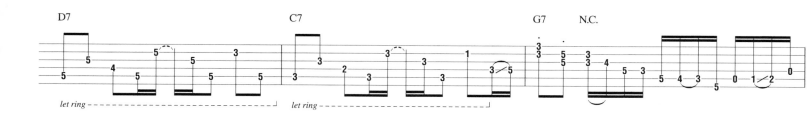

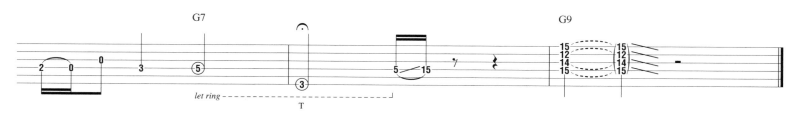